How Do We Move?

Carol Ballard

WAYLAND

How Our Bodies Work

How Do Our Eyes See?

How Do Our Ears Hear?

How Do We Taste and Smell?

How Do We Feel and Touch?

How Do We Think?

How Do We Move?

Editor: Ruth Raudsepp
Illustrators: Kevin Jones Associates and Michael Courtney
Designer: Phil Jackson

First published in 1997 by Wayland Publishers Ltd, 61 Western Road,
Hove, East Sussex, BN3 1JD, England.
© Copyright 1997 Wayland Publishers Ltd

Find Wayland on the internet at http://www.wayland.co.uk

British Library Cataloguing in Publication Data
Ballard, Carol
How Do We Move? – (How Our Bodies Work)
1. Musculoskeletal system – Juvenile literature
2. Human mechanics – Juvenile literature
I. Title II. Jones, K. III. Courtney, M.
612.7

ISBN 0 7502 2071 6

Picture acknowledgements
The author and publishers thank the following for use of their photographs:
Bubbles 4, 16 (left), 26, 28; Eye Ubiquitous 7; Chris Fairclough 5; Zul Mukhida 18, 19, 23;
Natural History Museum 10; NHPA 11; Science Photo Library 15, 20, 27, 29;
Tony Stone 6, 12, 16 (right), 24; Wayland Picture Library *contents page, cover*, 9;
Zefa 13, 15 and 25.

The author and publishers wish to thank Zul Mukhida, Bridget Tily and
Justine Heathcote for their kind assistance with this book.

Typeset by Phil Jackson
Printed in Italy by G Canale & C. S. p. A.

Contents

Movement

Think of the activities we do every day, such as running and jumping, talking and laughing and eating and breathing. Each of these actions needs some sort of movement. For some movements, like jumping, our whole body has to move from one place to another. Others, like blinking an eyelid, need only a tiny movement.

▲
What is the smallest movement you can make?

◄ Even when we are asleep, our bodies are not still. Our hearts beat and our chests move up and down as we breathe.

We can decide whether or not to raise our hand or nod our head. Movements like these are under our control. Movements such as our heart beating are not under our control. They happen automatically without us thinking about them.

▲
Every part of your body moves when you jump.

Activities, such as playing the violin, need several different movements to happen together. The fingers move individually, the arm moves to pull the bow backwards and forwards, and the eyes move to read the music. To **coordinate** these movements takes skill and practise.

You have to coordinate several ▶ different movements to play the violin.

Bones and Muscles

The human body contains two hundred and six bones and more than six hundred **muscles**. These bones and muscles allow us to move.

Bones are strong and hard and they can only bend a very small amount. Movement of bones can only happen where two bones meet. They cannot move themselves; they have to be pulled by muscles.

▲
Bones come in many shapes and sizes. This girl is looking at her hand which contains many small bones.

◀ It takes a lot of exercise to develop large, powerful muscles like these.

Imagine a horse pulling a cart. The cart cannot move itself, but the horse can pull it along the road. As it pulls, the horse uses energy and supplies power. Bones and muscles work in the same sort of way. The bone is like the cart, unable to move itself, and the muscle is like the horse, supplying the energy needed to pull the bone into a new position.

▲ This cart will not move until the horse pulls it along.

The Skeleton

The skeleton is a strong framework of bones. It gives the body shape, and supports all the other parts of the body. It allows us to stand upright and to move.

The brain is safe ▼ inside the strong bones of the skull.

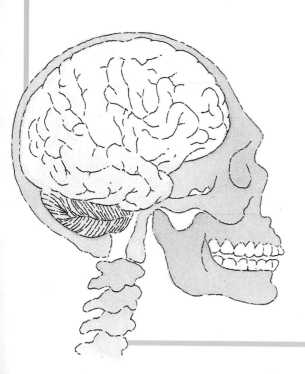

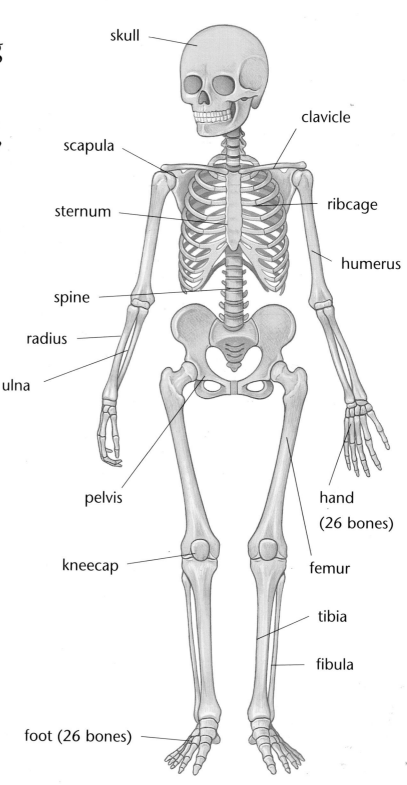

skull

clavicle

scapula

sternum

ribcage

spine

humerus

radius

ulna

pelvis

hand
(26 bones)

kneecap

femur

tibia

fibula

foot (26 bones)

The skeleton also
protects the body parts.
The brain, eyes and ears
are protected by the skull
bones. The heart and
lungs are protected by
the ribcage. The spine forms a strong,
bony tube, protecting bundles of **nerves** inside.

The longest, heaviest and strongest bone in the
body is the femur or thigh bone. It measures about
one quarter of our height. The smallest bones in
the body are the ossicles
inside the inner part
of the ears.

◀ A bendy backbone
allows us to twist our
bodies in all directions.

Inside a Bone

Bones need to be strong enough to support our weight. They also need to be light so that we can move around easily.

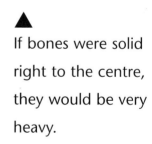

spongy bone

Bones are made of living **cells**, like the rest of the body. There are several different layers that make up a bone. The outer layer of a bone is like a tough, hard case. This protects everything inside it. It contains nerves and **blood vessels.**

▲ If bones were solid right to the centre, they would be very heavy.

10

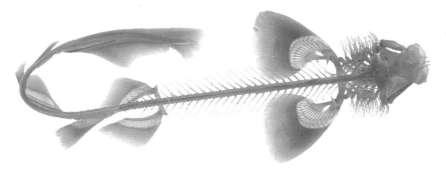

◀ This is the skeleton of a dogfish. Its bones are made of a softer, rubbery material called **cartilage.**

The next layer is a very strong, hard layer called compact bone. Holes run through the compact bone layer to carry nerves and blood vessels to the centre of the bone.

Beneath the compact bone is a light layer called spongy bone. This spongy bone is like a honeycomb. The spaces are full of a soft jelly called bone marrow.

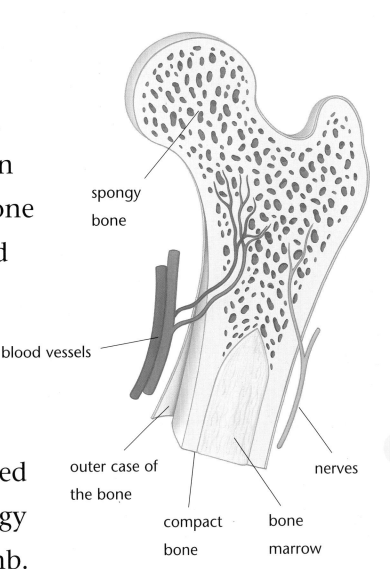

spongy bone

blood vessels

outer case of the bone

nerves

compact bone

bone marrow

▲ This is what a bone looks like inside.

◀ Some creatures, like this beetle, have skeletons outside their body. These are made of a hard, strong material called chitin.

Joints

A **joint** is the place where two bones meet. At some joints, the bones fit tightly together and cannot move. The bones in your skull have fixed joints which cannot move.

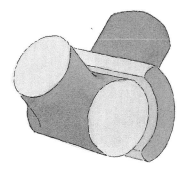

▲ Your elbow joint allows your arm to bend up and down.

Some joints, such as your elbow, only allow the bones to move in one direction. These joints are called hinge joints, because they work like the hinges of a door.

◀ Your shoulder joint lets you move your arm around in all directions.

Other joints, such as your shoulder and hip, allow movements in more directions. These joints are called ball and socket joints. The end of one bone forms a hole in which the ball-head of the other bone can swivel and turn easily.

Hurdlers must have very supple hip joints.

The ends of bones need to be protected so that they do not rub against each other as they move. They are covered with a layer of **cartilage**. Strong cords called **ligaments** hold the joint together. A layer of fluid acts like oil, allowing smooth movements of joints.

The only bone in your head which ▶ moves is your lower jaw. The rest fit together like pieces from a jigsaw.

Muscles

There are three main types of muscle in your body.

The muscles of your heart are specially designed to be able to work all the time without getting tired.

Circular muscles form strong elastic rings which control the size of openings such as your lips.

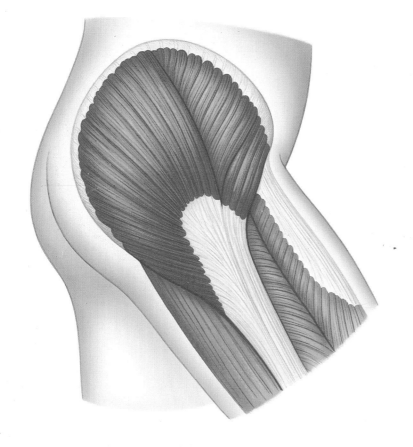

◀ The biggest and strongest muscles in the body are the buttock muscles. They move the hips and legs.

Muscles that let you move are attached to bones. These muscles are made of rows of **fibres.** Under a microscope, these rows of muscle fibres make the muscle look stripy.

This photograph of muscle fibres was taken while looking down a microscope.

Muscles are attached to bones by strong cords called **tendons.** Some muscles are attached by a single tendon, others are attached by many tendons. The tendons which need to be very strong, such as those joining the upper arm muscle to the shoulder blade, have a wide fan of tendons.

Strong leg muscles push ▶ this athlete forward.

Moving Bones

Muscles usually work in pairs. Each muscle of a pair has the opposite effect to the other muscle.

The end of each muscle is attached to a different bone. Muscles work by getting shorter or contracting. When a muscle **contracts**, it pulls one bone towards the other bone.

▲
Using a computer keyboard needs small, coordinated movements.

◀ Fast or slow, all our movements rely on pairs of muscles.

A contracted muscle cannot stretch itself out again. It has to be stretched back by the other muscle. This means that a muscle can only pull bones, it cannot push them.

When you nod your head, a muscle under your chin contracts, pulling your head forwards and down. A muscle at the back of your neck is stretched. To lift your head, the opposite happens. The muscle in the back of your neck contracts, pulling your head backwards and up, and the muscle under your chin stretches.

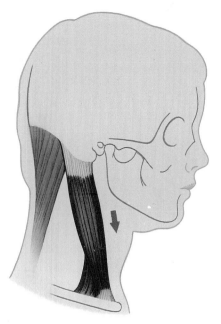

Muscle under the chin contracts and muscle in the neck is stretched. The head drops forward.

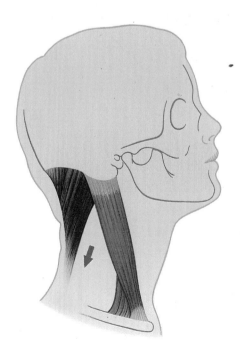

Muscle in the neck contracts and muscle under the chin stretches. The head lifts.

Model Muscles

Make this model to see how muscles move bones.

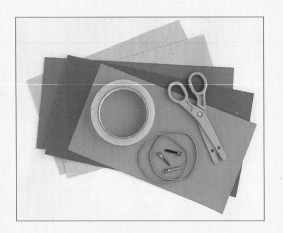

Step 1

You will need some stiff card, two elastic bands, sticky tape, split pins and a pair of scissors.

Step 2

Make a template of the shoulder, upper arm bone and lower arm bone out of stiff card. Using the template draw and cut the shoulder, upper arm bone and lower arm bone out of blue, red and green card.

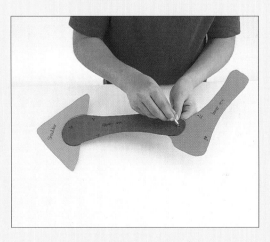

Step 3

Stick the upper arm into place at the shoulder with sticky tape. Fasten the joints of the upper arm bone and lower arm bone with the split pin. Leave the joints loose enough for the bones to move freely.

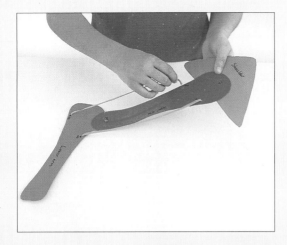

Step 4

Cut the elastic bands to make two straight pieces of elastic. Put the end of an elastic band through a small hole at one side of the upper arm bone. Position the bones so that they are at right angles to each other. Without stretching the elastic band put the other end through a small hole at the top of the lower arm. Put the other elastic band through a hole at the other side of the upper arm and through a hole on the lower arm as shown in the photograph. Secure the ends of the elastic bands with sticky tape.

19

Step 5

Gently pull the lower arm bone and watch what happens to the elastic muscles of the upper arm.

How Muscles Work

Every muscle is linked to your brain by a network of nerves. Messages travel to and from your brain along the nerves. When you want to raise your hand, for example, a message travels from your brain to the muscle in your arm. The muscle gets the message and contracts. This contraction pulls the bone and your hand is raised.

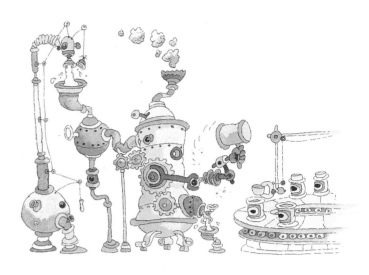

▲
Muscles are like machines; they use energy and make waste products.

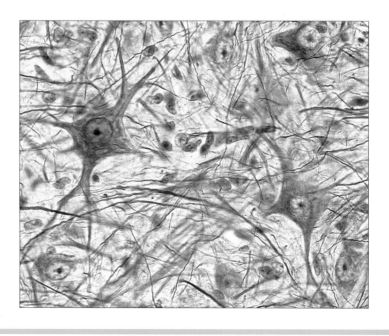

The nerve cells are the brown star shaped bodies with fibres leading off them. Nerves carry messages from the brain to the muscles. ▶

20

Each muscle is made up of millions of tiny fibres. There are two different types of muscle fibre. When a muscle gets the message to contract, these fibres slide over each other, making the muscle shorter and fatter.

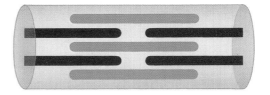

▲ When muscle contracts muscle fibres slide past each other.

▲ When muscle stretches muscle fibres slide back again.

When the bone is pulled back in the opposite direction, the muscle is stretched. The fibres slide back over each other in the opposite direction, making the muscle longer and thinner.

Muscles use energy when they contract. They also make waste products. Blood transports energy to the muscles and takes waste products away.

Muscles at Work

Try this activity with a friend and watch your muscles work.

Stand with your arm stretched out in front of you, with your palm facing upwards. Ask your friend to measure round the fattest part of your upper arm and the fattest part of your lower arm. Record the measurements. When your friend puts the book on your palm, bend your elbow to a right angle and lift the book upwards. Hold it still while your friend takes the measurements of your upper arm and lower arm again.

▲
This boy's leg muscles work hard, stretching and contracting as he jumps.

Did you find that your upper arm became fatter when you were holding the book in the air? This is because the upper arm muscle contracts to pull the lower arm bone upwards.

Did your lower arm muscle become fatter when your arm was horizontal? The lower arm muscle contracts to pull the bone down.

◄ These children are finding out which muscles in the arm get shorter and fatter when the book is lifted upwards.

Look After Your Muscles

To stay fit and healthy it is important to exercise regularly. Muscles which are not used can become weak. Exercise strengthens all the muscles and bones in the body, including the heart muscle. Swimming, cycling, dancing and football help you stay fit and can be great fun too.

▲ Slouching on a sofa is not good for muscles or bones, and causes backache.

◀ Swimming is very good exercise. It uses many muscles and makes the heart and lungs work hard too.

Eating a well-balanced diet is important. Milk, yoghurt and cheese are rich in calcium, which helps to strengthen bones. Meat, fish, eggs and nuts are rich in protein which helps to build strong muscles.

▲ These foods are rich in calcium which adds strength to bones.

The way we move, sit, lift and carry objects affects our muscles and bones. To keep muscles and bones in good condition, try to sit up instead of slouching on a sofa. When picking something up from the floor, remember to bend your knees instead of your back.

Broken Bones

Bones are strong, but they can break.

James fell off a swing and landed awkwardly on his arm. His arm hurt and he could not move it properly. His mother told him to keep it still and together they went to the hospital.

Even knights protected their heads – it makes sense to do the same!

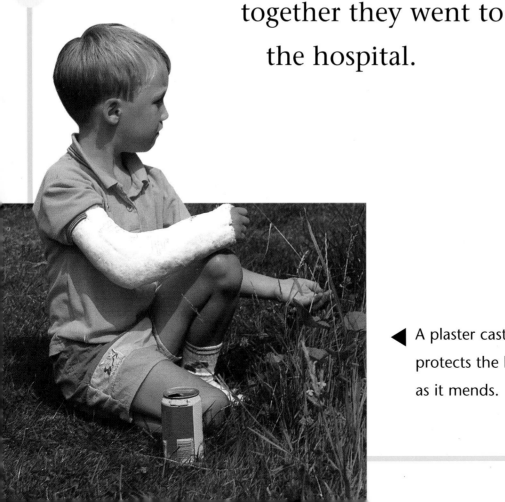

◀ A plaster cast protects the bone as it mends.

James's arm was X-rayed
and it showed that
the bone was broken.
The doctor straightened
James's broken bone and
then wrapped a plaster
bandage from his fingers
to his elbow.

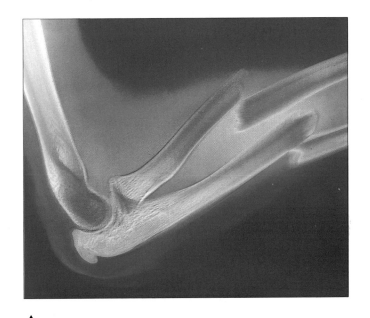

▲

This X-ray shows the doctor where the
bones in the arm are broken.

The plaster bandage turned hard as it dried, and
kept James's arm straight and still.

Over the next few weeks, new bone will grow,
joining the broken ends together. James will
keep the plaster on his arm until the bone
is completely mended. When the doctor takes
the plaster off, James's arm will be healed and
strong again.

When Things Go Wrong

Accidents and diseases can cause problems with muscles and bones.

A sprained ankle means that the tough ligaments holding the joint together are torn. The joint needs to be kept still until the ligaments heal.

▲
Athletes can suffer from tired painful muscles and have to stop training.

If the two bones at a joint are forced apart, the joint is **dislocated**. This happens most often at the arm and shoulder joint. Doctors can usually ease the bone back into position.

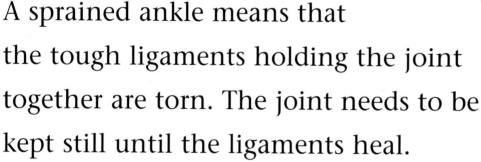

◀ Bandaging a sprained ankle will provide support until it has healed.

Between each bone in the **spine** are small discs of cartilage. Sometimes, one of these discs gets squeezed out of place. This is called a slipped disc. It can be painful, but can usually be put right by rest and gentle exercises.

Disc in normal position

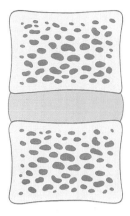

Disc that has slipped out of position

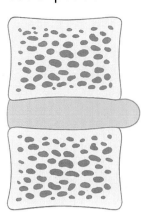

▲
Awkward movements can cause a disc of cartilage in the spine to move out of line.

Arthritis is a disease which affects the joints. The joints become swollen, stiff and painful, and movement can become difficult.

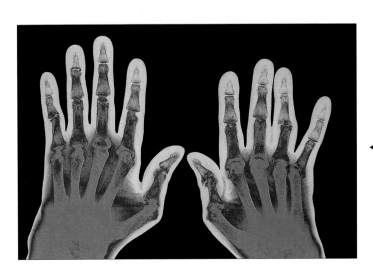

◄ This coloured X-ray shows the hands of a person with arthritis. The joints are swollen and some of the fingers are bent because of the swelling.

Glossary

blood vessels A network of tubes through which blood flows around your body.

cartilage A rubbery-like body tissue.

cells Millions of tiny building blocks that make up your body.

contracts Gets shorter.

coordinate Getting different movements to work together.

dislocated When a bone at a joint moves out of its normal position.

fibres Long, thread-like cells.

joint The junction where two bones meet.

ligaments Tough cords that hold a joint together.

muscles Bundles of fibres which contract or relax to move bones.

nerves Cells which carry messages between your brain and the rest of your body.

spine The backbone made of separate bones which support the body, but allow it to bend.

tendons Tough cords attaching a muscle to a bone.

Books to Read

For younger readers

Skeletons and Movement (Simple Science series) by Maria Gordon (Wayland, 1994).

Your Body: Bones by Anna Sandeman (Franklin Watts, 1997).

For older readers

The Skeleton and Muscular System by Carol Ballard The Human Body series (Wayland, 1997).

The Skeleton and Movement by Brian Ward Human Body series (Franklin Watts, 1997).

Index